IMAGES
of America

HAMILTON FIELD

IMAGES
of America

HAMILTON FIELD

Novato Historical Guild

ARCADIA
PUBLISHING

Published by Arcadia Publishing
Charleston, South Carolina

Library of Congress Catalog Card Number: 2008924124

For all general information contact Arcadia Publishing at:
Telephone 843-853-2070
Fax 843-853-0044
E-mail sales@arcadiapublishing.com
For customer service and orders:
Toll-Free 1-888-313-2665

Visit us on the Internet at www.arcadiapublishing.com

*To Lt. Col. William Palmer, USAF retired, and his wife, Irene, who first
organized the Hamilton Collection of the Novato History Museum, and
to the men and women who served, worked, and lived at Hamilton Field.*

CONTENTS

ACKNOWLEDGMENTS

Since its inception in 1976, so many volunteers of the Novato Historical Guild have contributed their time and skills to keep Novato's history alive that it would be impossible to thank everyone who has had a role in preserving our local history. The Novato Historical Guild, in cooperation with the City of Novato, operates the Novato History Museum. Lt. Col. William "Bill" R. Palmer, retired U.S. Air Force (USAF), Irene Palmer, and Leonard Benaski documented and organized hundreds of photographs and archival documents to create the museum's Hamilton Room. Because of their work, this book is possible. Unless otherwise noted, all images and archival material used in this book are from the collection of the Novato History Museum.

Novato Historical Guild members formed an author team to compile this book. Pat Johnstone, Edna Manzoni, Jim McNern, Elayne Miller, Michael Read, Ron Vela, Iva Young, and Samantha Kimpel, museum curator, contributed research, chose images, and wrote and edited text. The following staff, volunteers, and guild members contributed research, ideas, and editing assistance for this book: Bill Almeida, Dick Altman, Kay Antongiovanni, Margaret Binggeli, Bob Douglass, Ray Dwelly, Roland Fuette, Diana Goebel, Kathy Graves, Dottie Hicks, Dan Johnstone, Bob Manzoni, Glen Myers, Mike Silva, John Trumbull, May Ungemach, Pat Willat, Judy Walker, and Novato High School students Jessica Lehane and Danielle Moeller. The authors also gratefully acknowledge the City of Novato for its support of museum and guild projects. Arcadia editor John Poultney was instrumental in encouraging this project to come to fruition.

And finally, the authors want to extend special thanks to the past and present board of directors of the Novato Historical Guild for their support of this project, as well as for their continued support for the future Hamilton Field History Museum.

INTRODUCTION

In the late 1920s, the U.S. War Department actively built new facilities on the West Coast and announced the intention to build a new air base in California. A committee was formed to lobby to bring the new facility to Marin County. The Marin Board of Supervisors—through a county tax increase and contributions from other communities—purchased 937 acres in Novato at the edge of San Pablo Bay, which the county then sold to the government for $1. Construction began in 1932, and the base was built in three years for a cost of $5 million. In 1933, $3.6 million of this cost was funded from the Public Works Administration. As a result, many local laborers were employed during the height of the Depression.

Construction engineer was Capt. Howard Nurse. In acknowledgement of the Mediterranean climate and Spanish-American heritage of the area, Nurse designed the architecture in a combination Spanish-American Colonial Revival and art moderne style. The post was designed as a self-contained village with a post exchange, commissary, barber and beauty shops, cleaners, two theaters, two pools, and recreation facilities.

The base was named the Hamilton Army Airfield (AAF) for Lt. Lloyd Andrews Hamilton, a World War I pilot, the first American officer to fly with the British Royal Flying Corps, and the first in his squadron to shoot down an enemy plane. He was killed in combat after four months in action and received the Distinguished Service Cross posthumously.

The base was dedicated by Brig. Gen. Hap Arnold, commander of all western U.S. Army Air Corps activities, and Gov. Frank Merriam of California on May 12, 1935. The field was established as one of the only three in the United States to headquarter the 1st Wing of the Army Air Force. At that time, the base runway was suitable for B-12 and B-18 bombers. Pursuit planes were also sent to Hamilton AAF in the years leading up to World War II, including P-36s and P-40s, and the base was also home of the 10th Pursuit Wing.

During World War II, Hamilton AAF was the major link for U.S. Army Air Corps activities in the Pacific theater. Maj. Richard Bong, who trained at the base in P-38s, became the all-time top U.S. fighter ace with 40 Japanese aircraft destroyed. Hamilton AAF was also headquarters for the Pacific Division of the Air Transport Command, as well as the main evacuation station for wounded and released prisoners of war. As many as 4,000 patients per month—mainly from the Pacific theater—came through and were treated at Hamilton AAF at the height of the war. The first United Nations Conference on International Organization was held in San Francisco in April 1945, and many of the delegates were officially received at Hamilton AAF, including Pres. Harry Truman.

The end of the war in Europe came on May 7, 1945, with the unconditional surrender of the Germans, but the war in the Pacific had not yet been won. Before the fighting ended on August 14, 1945, the Atomic Age was ushered in by the bombs that fell on Hiroshima and Nagasaki, Japan. Hamilton AAF played a part in delivering the atomic bomb. A convoy consisting of a closed truck and seven cars with security agents left Sante Fe for Albuquerque, New Mexico. The pay load was flown from Kirkland Air Base to Hamilton Field. The manifest for the cargo was as follows: projectile assembly of active material for the gun type bomb; special tools and scientific instruments; inert parts for a complete gun type bomb; and uranium-235, half the fissionable amount available in the United States, valued at that time at $300 million. From Hamilton Field, the cargo traveled by armed convoy to Hunter's Point Naval Shipyard, where the USS *Indianapolis* transported it to Tinian in the Asian Pacific.

When the U.S. Air Force was created in 1947, the base was renamed Hamilton Air Force Base (AFB). During the years 1946–1960, Hamilton housed the headquarters for the 4th Air Force. During the Korean and Vietnam Wars, Hamilton AFB continued to be used as a training facility and was home to numerous fighter groups and air divisions. The base was home to the North American Aerospace Defense Command (NORAD) for western operations from 1966 to 1969, and was home to U.S. Air Force reserve units. However, the base did not serve as an evacuee hospital after the 1960s. Finally, due to changing national air defense missions and community concerns over the noise and safety of the base, the base was decommissioned in 1974 and vacated by 1975.

After deactivation, which coincided with the end of the Vietnam War, the base was used as an introduction center for refugees arriving from Southeast Asia. Over 180,000 Vietnamese, Cambodian, and Laotian refugees passed through Hamilton Field on their way to a new life in the United States up through the early 1980s. In the late 1980s, the base was used to produce Wings of Victory air shows.

Currently, Hamilton Field is the site of redevelopment and reuse. A number of architecturally important buildings have been declared part of a noncontiguous national historic district and have been preserved. They are either owned by the City of Novato or private developers. Housing developments are also part of that fabric, as are corporate headquarters of many national and international companies (from Birkenstock USA to Smith and Hawken) that now occupy renovated airplane hangars. The California State Coastal Conservancy is working on a project to restore the wetlands on the eastern portion of the base, including the former runway areas.

The Novato Historical Guild, along with the City of Novato, is currently preserving and renovating the former base firehouse, which will open as the Hamilton Field History Museum in 2009. The museum's mission is to collect, exhibit, and preserve materials that represent the history of the military groups and civilian communities of Hamilton. This mission will also help to communicate the role of Hamilton Field in the historical development of Marin County, as well as its role in the preservation of world peace.

One

FOUNDING AN ARMY AIRFIELD

On the western shore of San Pablo Bay, the fields managed by the California Packing Company were cultivating peas, sugar beets, and hay, and thus were given the name "Pea Patch." The photograph was labeled by hand A through E. Just above the "A" are the waters of San Pablo Bay (the northern portion of San Francisco Bay), with Black Point on the horizon. The first knoll in the right foreground became the site of the hospital. The second holds the officers' club. The main base would later be placed about where the "E" is located, and the runway would be placed on the field labeled "D."

In February 1929, Col. G. C. C Brant led a flight of five planes to Marin Meadows, later reporting the site entirely suitable for an airfield. Pictured from left to right are pilot (unidentified); L. C. Smith; Robert N. Carson; Congressman James; Clarence F. Lea, Congressman, 1st District for California; Col. Brant, Commander of San Francisco's Crissy Field; and William Deysher, Marin County Supervisor. The aircraft is an Atlantic C-2 Tri Motor.

In 1931, the secretary of war announced that the new airfield would be named in honor of 1st Lt. Lloyd Andrews Hamilton. Hamilton was born in Troy, New York, on June 13, 1894. Hamilton enlisted in the U.S. Army on April 28, 1917, and was commissioned 1st Lieutenant on March 2, 1918. He was assigned to the front in France and was attached to the famous British 3rd Aero Squadron. The first American to fly with the Royal Flying Corps, he was transferred to the U.S. Air Service on June 20, 1918, and became the Flight Commander of the 17th Aero Squadron. He received the Distinguished Flying Cross at Varssonaore, Belgium, for "Extraordinary Heroism in Action" on August 13, 1918. He was killed in action near Lagnecourt, France, 13 days later, on August 26, 1918.

Henry Greer hands over the deed to the army on March 17, 1932. After negotiations, the California Packing Company agreed to sell 776 acres for $174 an acre. When that amount of acreage proved to be inadequate, they discovered that Dr. Bodkin, owner of the adjacent land, was asking $600 an acre. Eventually Bodkin agreed to sell for $300 an acre.

On April 28, 1931, Capt. Howard B. Nurse, U.S. Army Quartermaster Corps, arrived at the site to handle construction bids. Captain Nurse thoughtfully designed Hamilton Field as a beautiful place in which to work and live. Captain Nurse envisioned the base to be built emphasizing the Spanish/Mexican influence predominant in California's history.

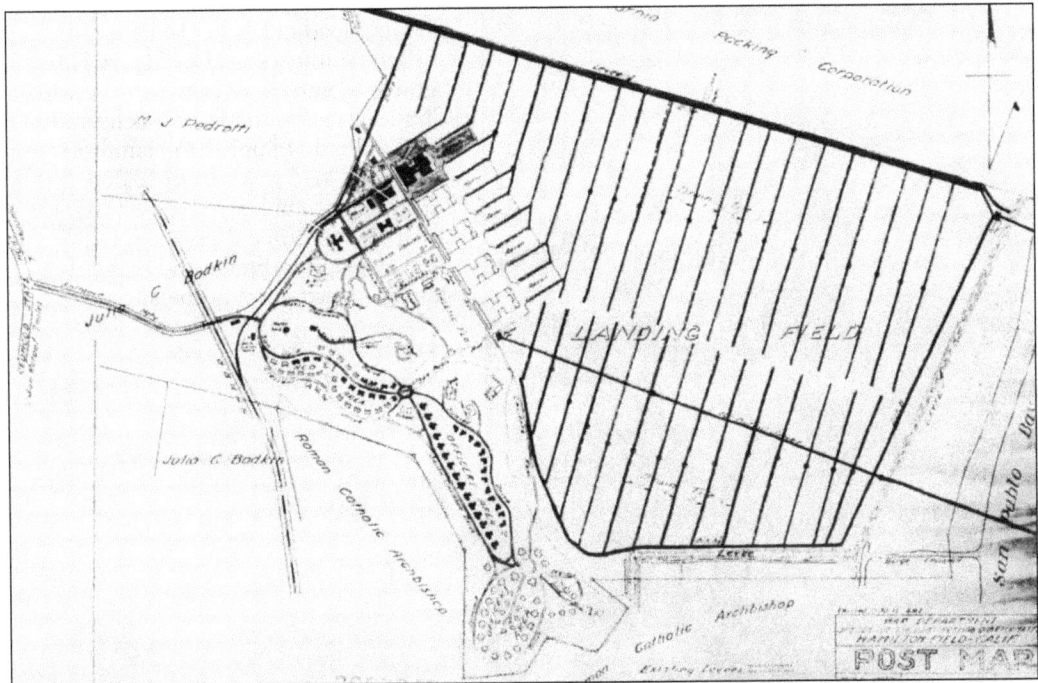

These plans were dated November 30, 1932. They showed the roads, the layout of the drainage system, and the location of the hangars, barracks, and administration building, as well as enlisted and officer housing. Also the plans indicate individual landowner parcels.

An aerial photograph taken in June 1932 shows the preliminary work being done on the roads into and around the flat lands of the airbase. Hamilton Field is ideally located from a military point of view. It is strategically located about halfway between the Canadian and Mexican borders, enabling a quick dispatch to all Pacific Coast points.

The first load of lumber is delivered to the Hamilton site. The Henry Hess Lumber Company of San Rafael—with Charles Lund as manager—delivered the first load of lumber to Hamilton Field. The load was part of 10,000 linear feet of lumber to be used to construct an office that would be used by Captain Nurse and his staff during construction of the airbase.

Hamilton Field has many palm trees lining the street from the front gate to the headquarters buildings. This tree was donated by the Vanderbilt family of San Rafael and is in transit to Hamilton.

14

Construction throughout Hamilton moved quickly. Pictured here are some of the officers' living quarters under construction. The houses were designed in the Spanish style of architecture Captain Nurse had envisioned. Some of the homes being built for the upper command officers rivaled those built in the finest sections of San Francisco.

By mid-1933, construction was in full swing, and many of the roads, one of the enlisted men's barracks, one airplane shop, two hangars, and many support structures were well on their way to completion.

3-4-34. HAMILTON FIELD, CALIF.

Hamilton Field is seen here as it looked when the 7th Bombardment Group first occupied the airbase under the command of Lt. Col. Clarence L. Tinker. During the initial survey and study, it was stated that the climate in the Hamilton Field area is ideal for flying, providing at least 250 clear days a year, with no rainfall taking place from June to September. Normal rainfall is 25 inches per year. The annual mean temperature is 56.3 degrees, with average temperature of a minimum 40 degrees, maximum 63 degrees from October to April inclusive, and minimum 47 degrees, maximum 79 degrees from May to September inclusive.

Two

THE BOMBER BASE YEARS

In the haste to build the base and get the 7th Bombardment Group settled, no one had thought about formally dedicating the field. This oversight was remedied on May 12, 1935, when official ceremonies were held. Thousands of people turned out to see California governor Frank Merriam (left) turn over the new post to the U.S. Army. At the ceremony, Brig. Gen. Henry "Hap" Arnold (right), commander of all western U.S. Army Air Corps activities, noted that "Hamilton Field stands today as the most modern and best equipped, up-to-date military airfields in the United States." He thanked the public-spirited citizens of marvelous Marin who seven years prior envisioned a great flying field. Aviation history was made that day, during dedication festivities, with the first known aircraft-to-ground radio communication in U.S. Army Air Corps history by Lt. Col. Clarence L. Tinker, Hamilton Field commanding officer.

On March 3, 1935, the American Legion, fifth district, dedicated a bronze plaque honoring Lieutenant Hamilton, for whom the field had been named. The plaque was set in a large boulder that surfaced during field excavation, and the boulder was placed at the then main gate. In 1944, the bronze plaque was reset at the base of the flagpole in front of the headquarters building.

Maj. Gen. Paul B. Malone, 9th Corps Area Commander (left), arrived at Hamilton Field on April 6, 1935, to inspect the base on "Army Day." Standing next to him is Lt. Col. Clarence L. Tinker, Hamilton Field commanding officer. General Malone inspected the line of planes, personnel, and transportation for possible discrepancies. After inspection, there was an aerial review in his honor in which all of the combat planes passed in mass formation before him.

The U.S. Congressional Subcommittee on Appropriations met with General Malone and Colonel Tinker. From left to right are Tillman B. Parkes, Arkansas (chairman); Gen. P. B. Malone; John Dockweiler of California; J. Buell Snyder of Pennsylvania; Thomas Blanton of Texas; Colonel Tinker; and T. McMillan of South Carolina.

The first main gate to Hamilton Field in 1935 was just beyond the first bridge, on Main Entrance Road, near the railroad crossing. The guardhouse has been preserved and currently stands in about the same location. On top of the hill, commonly referred to as "Reservoir Hill," is a water tank and radio antenna. Both structures still remain on the hill.

This April 8, 1935, photograph of Hamilton Field is as it looked at time of dedication. Note the tall flagpole in front of Building 500 (headquarters building) and the single tall palm in the center of the road at the apex of the arc in the road. Running diagonally in the foreground is the rail spur servicing the maintenance facilities at the left. Behind the headquarters building are three enlisted men's barracks. A fourth barracks is to the right of the large open space used as a parade ground.

The houses—modern in appointment but Spanish in character—are scattered informally to take advantage of the approximately 1,000 full-grown oak trees that provide charm and shade. There are no fences, so each yard flows into the next. The higher-ranking officers were assigned to houses on higher elevations commanding spectacular views. Building complexity and decorative details decreased with decreasing rank.

This wood structure was the temporary headquarters of Capt. Howard B. Nurse, constructing quartermaster, during construction of Hamilton Army Airfield. The building later served as the first post chapel.

For recreation, the enlisted men could use this Olympic-size swimming pool, which was located across the street from the barracks. The pool was completed on September 17, 1934, at a cost of $9,108.50. It was called "Auxiliary water storage tank #1" in the plans and specs book on Hamilton Field.

In this aerial view, one can see the nine hangars. The double hangar buildings are identical H-shaped structures with a central shop area and hangars on either end. They are built of concrete covered with stucco. The single hangar has an attached office building and central control tower. The interior lobby of the control tower has elaborate Spanish Colonial elements, including tile stairways with decorative tile wainscoting, decorative metal railings, and metal light fixtures.

On December 1, 1934, the 7th Bombardment Group, which was stationed at March Field, California, began to move to its new permanent station at Hamilton Field. In this photograph, 24 of the 40 bombing planes and other aircraft had safely landed. A few days later the rest of the Martin B-10 bombers arrived. The remaining personnel came by train. The new contingent consisted of 48 officers, 30 flying cadets, and 522 enlisted men.

Seen here on January 28, 1935, are Martin B-12 bombers from Hamilton Field over San Francisco Bay. The twin-engine, dual-cockpit bombers were designed in 1932 and entered service in 1934 as B-10s. They differed from one another only in the type of engines that powered them: the B-10 was powered by the Wright Cyclone and the B-12 by the Pratt and Whitney engine. In the background is Yerba Buena Island. Work to build Treasure Island had yet to start.

In this May 3, 1935, aerial view of Hamilton Field, San Pablo Bay can be seen in the upper left-hand corner. California Packing Corporation owns the land in the lower left-hand corner, and the Roman Catholic Archdiocese owns the land in the upper right-hand corner. The officers' quarters on the hill are scattered informally to take advantage of the shade of the trees and of the wonderful view of San Pablo Bay.

In this January 10, 1936, photograph, Brig. Gen. Henry "Hap" Arnold (left) and Lt. Col. Clarence L. Tinker, base commander, are standing in front of a Martin bomber at Hamilton Field. On October 15, 1942, by command of Henry H. Arnold, commanding general of the U.S. Air Force, Tinker Air Force Base in Oklahoma was named in honor of Maj. Gen. Clarence L. Tinker, U.S. Army. He lost his life in the Battle of Midway. General Arnold took a deep and personal interest in Hamilton Field. He maintained quarters under the officers' club until his death in 1950.

Two of the Douglas B-7 observation planes of the 88th Observation Squadron, 7th Bombardment Group stationed at Hamilton Field fly in a sky parade and review of the 1st Wing. In 1936, six Douglas observation planes and their Fokker observation plane transferred to Hamilton Field from Brook Fields, Texas.

Martin B-12 bombers from Hamilton Field are on maneuvers over San Francisco, California, on January 28, 1936. The speedy Martin bombers were capable of a speed of 220 miles per hour and could carry up to 2,260 pounds of bombs. The Golden Gate Bridge under construction is in the background.

(G-100 32E-HP) (4-11-36-10:45A)   QUARTERLY LOAD TEST INSPECTION

Pilots and crewmembers of the 7th Bombardment Group are standing next to their assigned Martin bombers for the quarterly wing load test inspection. The pilot who controls the aircraft is an officer, usually a captain or lieutenant. Next in command is also an officer, the copilot, who is both an aviator and a bombing expert. The front gunner, who is also the crew chief and usually an enlisted man, sits in the transparent turret in front of the bomber between the engines. The fourth man is the radio operator, who is a soldier with a specialist rating. He also fires the bottom machine gun.

The U.S. Army blimp flies over Hamilton Field while the 7th Bombardment Group is inspected during the quarterly wing load test inspection on April 24, 1936.

At the time of its assignment at Hamilton Field, the 7th Bombardment Group had the 9th, 11th, and 31st Bombardment Squadrons assigned to it and the 70th Service Squadron. The 7th Bombardment Group and its tactical squadrons represented some of the most experienced units in the U.S. Army Air Corps. They were assigned to the 1st Wing to provide Pacific Coast defenses.

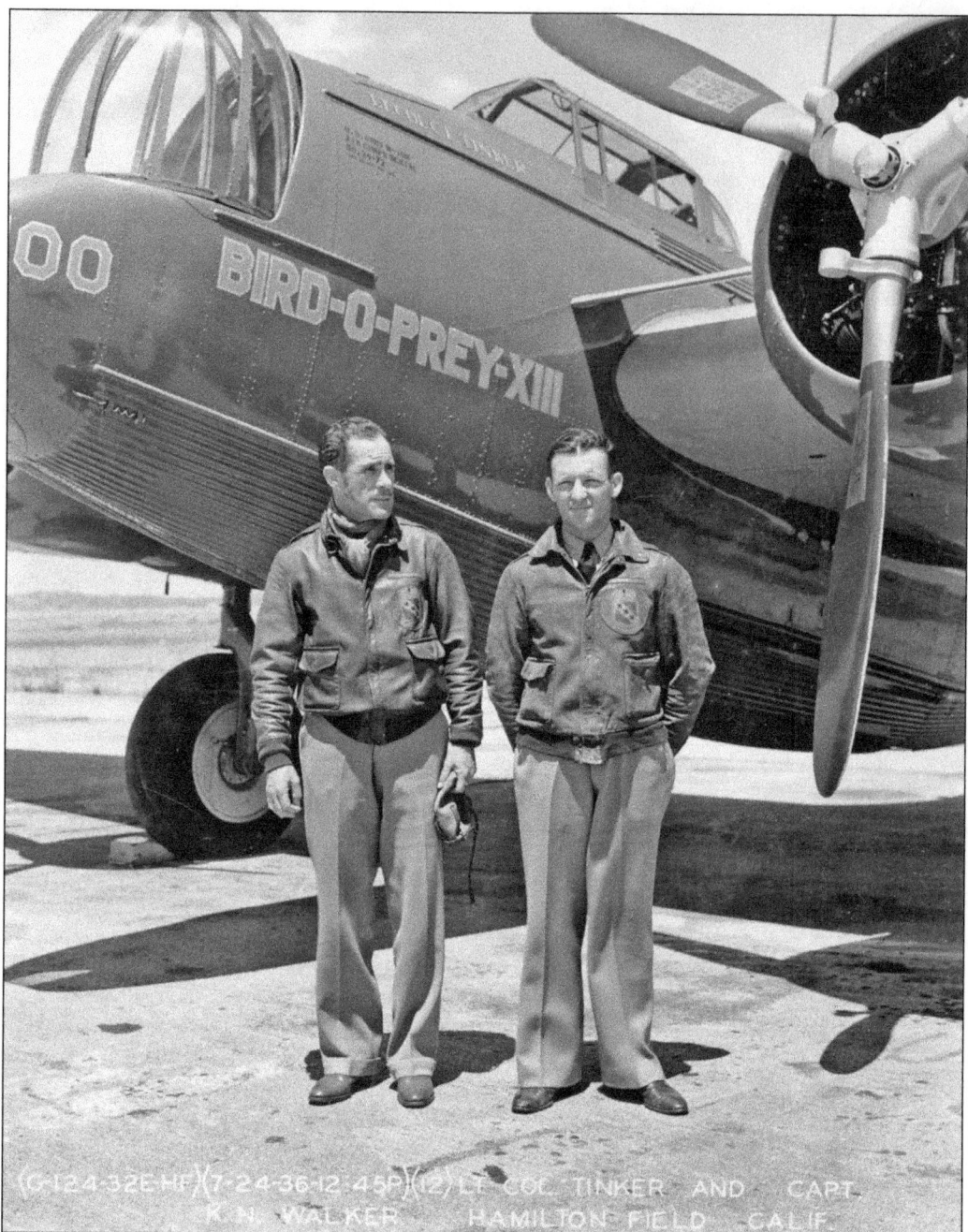

Lt. Col. Clarence L. Tinker, base commander (left) and Capt. K. N. Walker at Hamilton Field are standing in 1936 in front of Colonel Tinker's personal aircraft, a Martin B-10 bomber named "Bird-O-Prey-XIII." In November 1936, Lt. Col. George E. Stratemeyer took this plane on a practice flight. The airplane lost power while approaching Runway No. 30, and landed in three feet of water in upper San Pablo Bay. There were no injuries. The plane was only slightly damaged, thanks to the soft mud in which it landed, although salvaging the craft presented considerable difficulty.

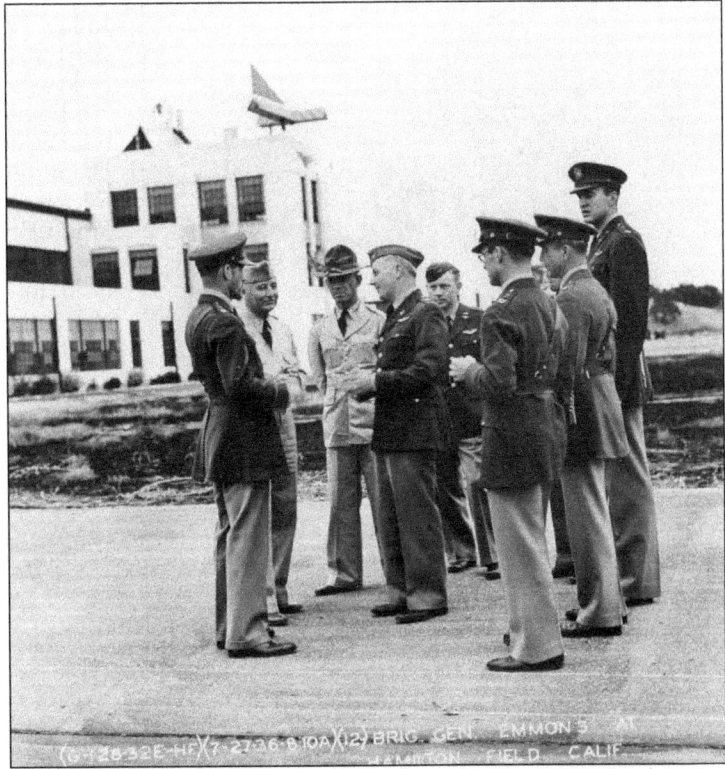

Brig. Gen. Delos Carleton Emmons (center) visits Hamilton Field on July 27, 1936. He had just become commander of the 1st Wing at March Field, California. He is talking to Col. Clarence L. Tinker (left), commander of Hamilton Field. They are standing in front of the three-story control tower that is attached to Hangar No. 7.

A review for Tinker's (front row, center) departure from Hamilton Field was held in December 1936. He became commander of Hamilton Field on December 5, 1934. Tinker was the first American general lost in World War II, and his body was never recovered. He was called, "an enlisted man's general" by the men who worked for him. General Tinker received the Distinguished Service Medal posthumously.

In July 1936, Col. Davenport Johnson (left) was transferred to Hamilton Field as commanding officer of the 7th Bombardment Group and later became commanding officer of Hamilton Field. Stratemeyer (right) was promoted to lieutenant colonel in June 1936 and assigned to command the 7th Bomb Group at Hamilton Field. In 1941, he became executive officer to Gen. Henry H. Arnold, the chief of the U.S. Army Air Corps.

Col. Gerald "Jerry" Brant (left) and Col. Davenport Johnson, commander of Hamilton Field, are seen here standing in front of Brant's personal aircraft. Brant served as commanding officer at Crissy Field, California, from 1927 to 1929. Colonel Johnson was the base commander at Hamilton Field from December 16, 1936, to February 25, 1938.

In this aerial photograph, one can see the 4,500-foot runway at Hamilton Field. The landing field was below sea level at high tide, so a levee was built around the field and a 3,700-foot dike was constructed along the bay front. A pumping station was built in 1933 to lift drainage water over the dike (lower left-hand corner) into San Pablo Bay. Another pumping station was built in 1940; each station had large pipelines located beneath the structures with pipelines extending east into the bay.

31

The Boeing B-17 Flying Fortress had a limited duration at Hamilton Field because these larger, faster, and heavier planes (larger than the B-12 or B-18) needed a longer and stronger runway.

B-17s are lined up on the Hamilton runway in the late 1930s. In 1939, the 7th Bombardment Group was designated a "heavy" bomb group and was moved to Fort Douglas, Utah, on September 7, 1940, to train with B-17s.

In this October 1939 photograph, B-18 Douglas Bombers from the 7th Bombardment Group are flying over Hamilton Field. These planes were phased into reconnaissance work when replaced by the B-17 for combat duty. The Douglas B-18 Bolos, shown below on the tarmac, replaced the 7th Bombardment Group's B-12 bombers in 1937.

The B-18 was a standard twin-engine, short-range bomber and was capable of airlifting combat-equipped troops en masse, which was an important advance in combat techniques at the time. (Courtesy of Col. William R. Palmer, retired USAF.)

The water-storage tank, on the hill to the left, overlooks the base and is used both as a water tank and beacon. It is about 60 feet high and has a capacity of 265,000 gallons. The red-and-white checkerboard paint job is evidence of its use as a visual landmark. The noncommissioned officers' (NCO) club is the building to the (front) right, and next to it is the base theater. The main gate is to the right of the bridge.

In this 1939 aerial photograph, one can see the recently completed taxiways upgraded for safety measures. Because the field was below sea level, the upper crust of earth would not support the aircraft if it ran over the end of a runway on landing. The plane would mire down or go over, causing damage to the plane. The new taxiways were also necessary for fast and efficient takeoffs and landings in formation.

In 1939, rows of wooden barracks (center) began to spring up on the base as Hamilton Field expanded to meet its new role as an important West Coast air-training facility. The need for more barracks led to the abandonment of Capt. Howard B. Nurse's construction plan for all Spanish-style buildings. This type of construction was to continue throughout the war years until the "Splinter City"–type housing (temporary wooden construction) far exceeded that of the original plan.

(G14-32E-HF)(2-28-35) HEADQUARTERS, HAMILTON FIELD

The headquarters building is the main administrative building on the base. The structure is T-shaped, with a central two-story building flanked by one-story wings. The two wings have end-gable roofs over mission arches that form an arcade, or covered walkway, ending in front gable roofs at either end. The entryway in the central facade has decorative arched cornicing and a circular vent containing a six-pointed star. Inside an impressive central lobby with many eclectic Spanish Colonial Revival elements greets the visitor. Cut metal lighting fixtures sport a U.S. Army Air Corps design motif. Three corridors radiate at right angles from the lobby, each one flanked by small rooms.

One of the earliest architecturally unique buildings on the base, the firehouse was the fire, police, ambulance, crash, and undertaker service center of the Hamilton community. It was completed on August 18, 1934, at a cost of $37,799.34. The ground floor area housed an ambulance, fire engines, and a crash truck with a traditional fireman's brass pole from the dormitory on the second floor.

In this view of the firehouse, one can see the guardhouse wing (on the right), where the prisoners were kept. Each of the cells had a bunk, basin, and toilet, and there was one solitary cell to the far right. The guards had a dormitory on the second floor with a stairway that connected them to the guardhouse.

On top of a long knoll, the base commander's residence (center) is the largest and most elaborate house on the base. It is an H-shaped house, with a hipped, mission tile roof above a decorative cornice. The living room has a pair of arched multi-pane windows that provide a spectacular view of San Pablo Bay. From that vantage point, the base commander can see the entire flying field, as well as the greater part of the residential section.

This Spanish Colonial Revival–style hospital (center) has 24-inch-thick concrete walls covered in stucco and is three stories high. The ground floor holds laboratories and an X-ray room, the second floor offices, and the third operating rooms. To the right of the hospital is the detachment barracks, and to the left is an amphitheater. In front of the amphitheater is the Olympic-size enlisted men's swimming pool.

The bachelor's officers' quarters is a three-story rectangular building with a cross gable roof. The central lower story is composed of five arched and bracketed bays that lead to a central garage. On the second story are 17 apartments, quarters for bachelor officers, and a dormitory for visiting officers. A large kitchen and dining room are also in the building.

The noncommissioned officers' (NCO) club was completed on November 29, 1939, at a cost of $33,338.81. It had asbestos shingles and wood floors. The first floor had a large dance floor, a barroom, a parlor, and a library. On the second floor were offices. On the hill behind the NCO club was the water storage tank.

There were originally four enlisted men's barracks (three remain today); each had a capacity of 200 men. They are three stories high and were built by the K. E. Parker Company in 1933 and 1934.

The H-shaped enlisted barracks (Building 442, shown in this photograph) have heavily ornamented front doors and two-story Baroque door embellishments at the central main entrance. Each barrack had a kitchen, dining hall, barbershop, and tailor shop.

Hamilton Field Theatre was completed on April 7, 1938, after the base opened, at a cost of $54,387.24. It has a tile roof, elaborate door and window surrounds, and decorative stucco vents. It had a capacity of 422.

The officers' mess, a rambling hacienda on the crest of a high ridge, looks eastward over the waters of San Pablo Bay to distant Mount Diablo. It reflects the older, simpler mission design, especially in the use of curvilinear gables. It was completed on September 7, 1934. Later it was called the officers' club.

This small radio building was completed on May 31, 1933, at a cost of $5,473.50. It was located directly south of the hospital at the bottom of "Radio Hill." It had a large operating room, a small power room, and quarters. Like the other buildings, it was designed for beauty as well as utility.

This postcard of Hamilton's NCO quarters is postmarked 1936. The quarters were of varying sizes and arrangements, from duplexes to townhouses—all in the Spanish eclectic style of the buildings completed in the mid-1930s.

Three

WORLD WAR II AND REORGANIZATION

With the armies of Japan and Germany moving into other countries, Hamilton became a secure base; all traffic was stopped, and destinations were checked if one was a visitor. Because of its location, the field became the jumping-off point for Pacific-bound units and for personnel ferrying aircraft and supplies. From early 1941 until December 19, 1944, Hamilton Field was designated as the point of departure for bombardment air echelons bound for the Pacific. Facilities at the base were used to preflight the units, and for maintenance and repairs on aircraft arriving from shakedown cruises, depots, or places of assembly. The crews were housed and fed and given the latest flight information.

The 680th Ordnance is shown ready to depart for the Philippines in October 1941. The first mass movement of the bombardment aircraft to the Philippines by way of Hawaii took place on May 13, 1941. At that time, 21 crews of the 19th Bombardment Group flying B-17D aircraft departed from Hamilton Field for Hawaii. On October 26, 1941, additional aircraft and crews departed for permanent assignment to the Philippines.

A maintenance crew poses in front of a B-17 bomber at Hamilton in 1941. In response to the growing crisis in the Pacific, in early December 1941, four Boeing B-17C Flying Fortresses and two new B-17E's of the 30th Bombardment Group were flying cross country from New Orleans, Louisiana. They stopped at Hamilton Field on their way to Hickam Army Airfield (AAF) in Hawaii. Their plans were to proceed on to Clark Army Airfield in the Philippines to reinforce the 19th Bombardment Group stationed there. After leaving Hamilton and flying all night, the bombers arrived over Oahu on the morning of December 7, 1941. They arrived at Pearl Harbor at the height of the Japanese air attack on Hawaii, which helped trigger American entry into World War II. Some of the planes managed to land at a short fighter strip at Haleiwa, one set down on a golf course, and the remainder landed at Hickam Field under the strafing of Japanese planes.

On December 8, 1941, the day after Pearl Harbor, Hamilton Field started disappearing under wartime camouflage. With the declaration of war, Hamilton rapidly expanded to a wartime status, with the construction of additional barracks, mess halls, administration buildings, a warehouse, a building to house Link Trainer flight simulators, schools, and other structures. In the center of this photograph is the headquarters building.

Through arrangements with the Associated Press, a Teletype machine was installed in the war room of the service club at Hamilton. The machine was in operation from 8:00 a.m. to 12:00 a.m. daily. As the news came off the Teletype machine, it was left on the roll for a half hour, and then it was removed and attached by bright colored ribbon to the theater-of-operations map that it concerned.

An enlisted man was assigned to the war room with the full-time job of keeping the maps up to date. He also installed maps of the Pacific and European theaters on billboard in major buildings on the base, which showed daily and weekly progress on the battlefronts. Another map of the world, 9 by 12 feet, covered one wall of the war room and was divided into theaters of operation. The special shoulder patches of all the U.S. Air Forces were placed in their appropriate locations on it.

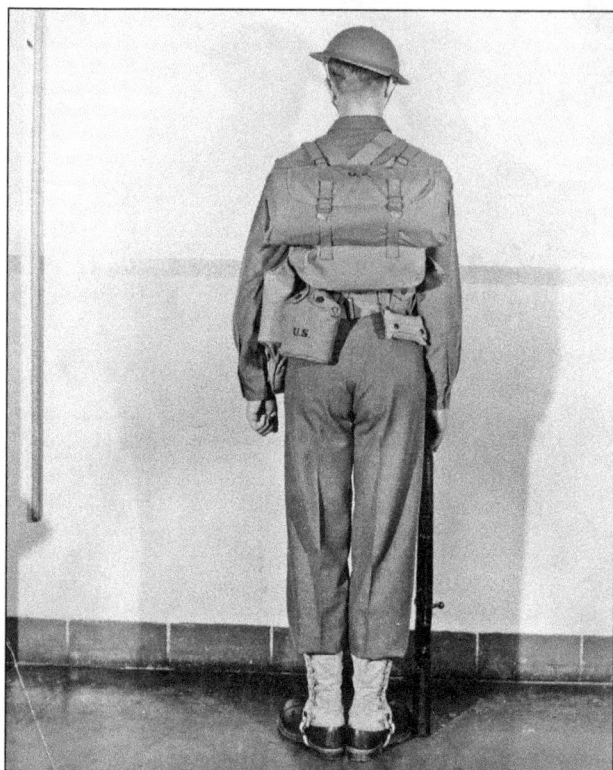

This photograph documents the uniform and how field equipment was assembled, worn, and carried by soldiers, April 21, 1942.

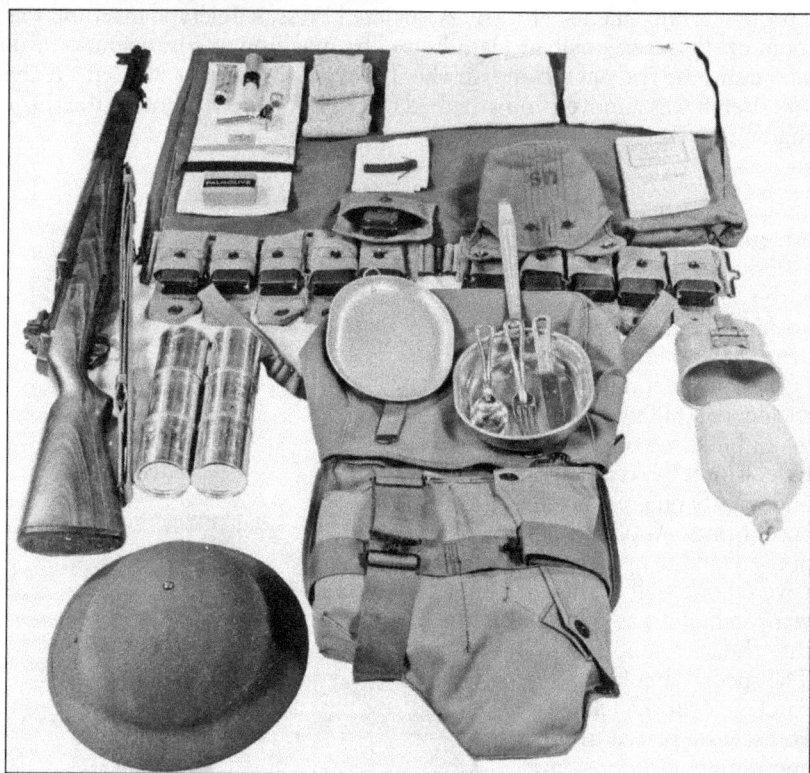

The personal kit for field soldiers included a helmet, rifle, ammunition, pocket tools, binoculars, food rations, water bottle, plate/cooking pan, silverware, socks, T-shirts, and personal toiletry items.

At the beginning of World War II, the U.S. Army Air Corps recognized its need for more ground-based trainers, or mechanical devices for pilot training. This was especially important for blind flying, which is instrument flying at night or in foul weather. Accordingly Hamilton Army Airfield was equipped with its first Link Trainers. The Link Trainers had a unique system of valves, levers, and vacuum bellows that simulated altitude, bank and pitch, air speed, and rough air. Trainees could feel these movements but could see only the illuminated instrument panel. This taught them to rely on their instruments to guide their responses to "blind" fight conditions. One of Hamilton's major roles in World War II was to train fighter pilots.

During World War II years, a number of newly formed fighter groups trained at Hamilton. The P-38 Lightning, shown on the Hamilton tarmac, was flown by the 78th, 329th, and 367th Fighter Groups, who trained at Hamilton from 1942 to 1943. (Courtesy of Col. William R. Palmer, retired USAF.)

The P-38, also known as the "Fork Tailed Devil," was a versatile aircraft that served in many roles: a high-altitude fighter, a dive bomber, a photograph and weather reconnaissance plane, a night fighter, a ground support aircraft, and as both a long-range bomber escort and pathfinder for B-17 bomb raids over most of Europe during World War II.

In 1942, the 328th Fighter Group was activated at Hamilton to replace the transferring 14th Fighter Group as part of the air defense force and also a group for replacement pilots in P-39 Airacobra, pictured here on the Hamilton tarmac. The P-39 was also flown by the 354th, the 363rd, and the 478th Fighter Groups who trained at Hamilton in 1942–1943.

The P-51 Mustang was flown by the 357th Fighter Group that trained at Hamilton in the mid-1940s. This long-range, single-seat fighter aircraft entered service in the Allied air forces in the middle years of World War II. The P-51 became one of the war's most successful and recognizable aircraft.

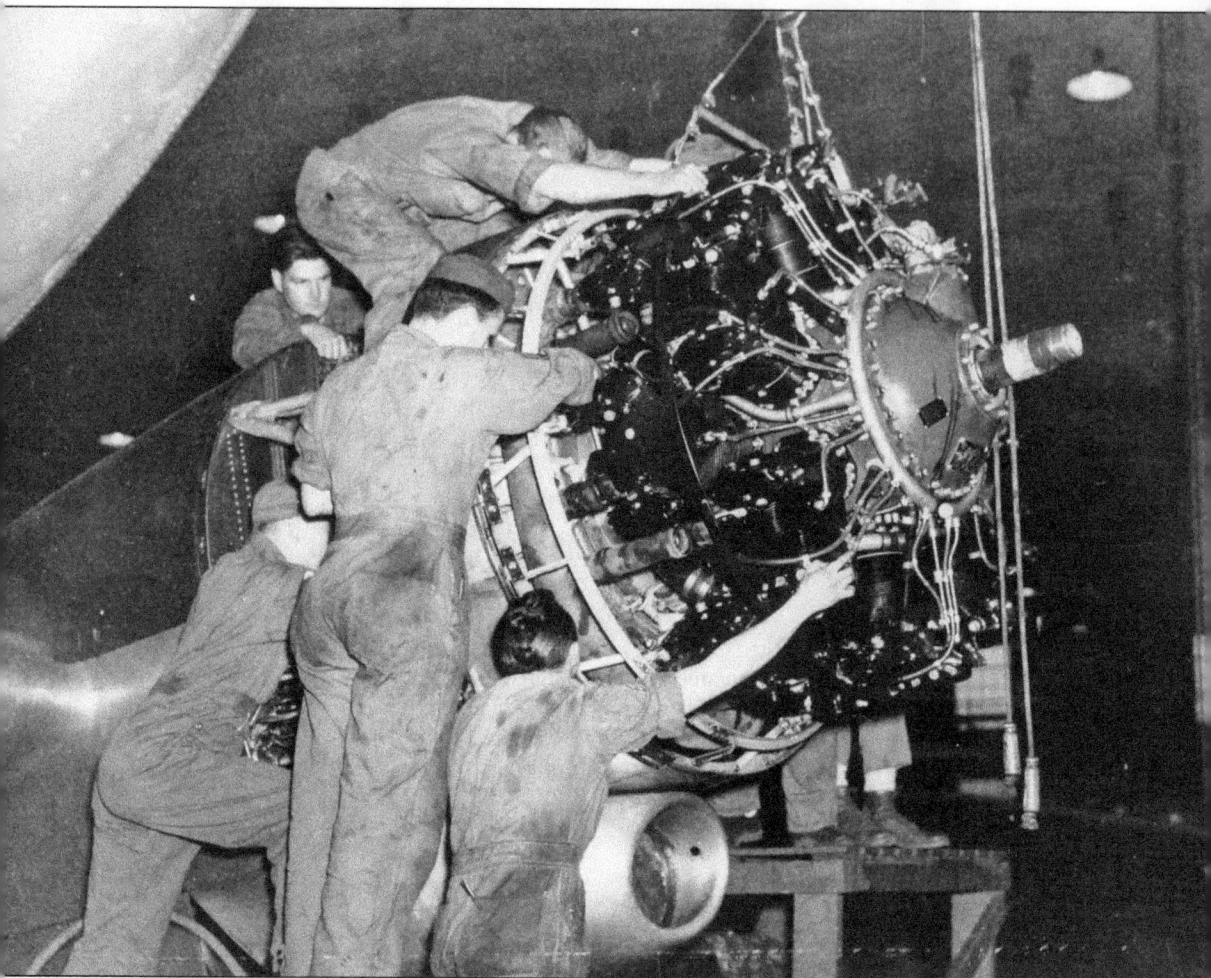

The dawn of any day at Hamilton field started with the bugler's blast, calling all personnel to get up. The drill was as follows: feet on the floor (the sound of foot and wall lockers banging), shower, shave, dress, make bed, shine shoes, dust lockers, arrange clothes, and sweep and mop under bed. Chow line was next, and the food was good and worth the wait: eggs, potatoes, cereal, jam toast, grapefruit, coffee, and milk—all for about 14¢. The days started at about 8:00 a.m., with each soldier and airman reporting to his assigned duties. An exception would be the flight line, and some emergency units that would be on 24-hour call, which would be covered in three 8-hour shifts. Here mechanics, photographed in 1946, kept the planes flying.

During the afternoon and night, the theater was used strictly for entertainment; however, during the morning hours, on many occasions, the theater was a site for briefing pilots, navigators, bombardiers, and crewmen, who marched to the theater in columns of fours. When the briefing for the morning was over, they marched away in the same formation.

These three airmen worked as projectionists at the Hamilton theater projection room. During World War II, every three months, the men and women of each squadron at Hamilton were required to report to the base theater to hear the reading of the Articles of War. The reading was intended to serve as a reminder to everyone that the United States was at war.

The base photo lab was an important part of documenting operations. The men and women who worked there were trained in four general phases of photography: basic principles; ground photography; aerial photography; and mosaic and mapmaking, all of which were essential tools in the U.S. Army Air Corps.

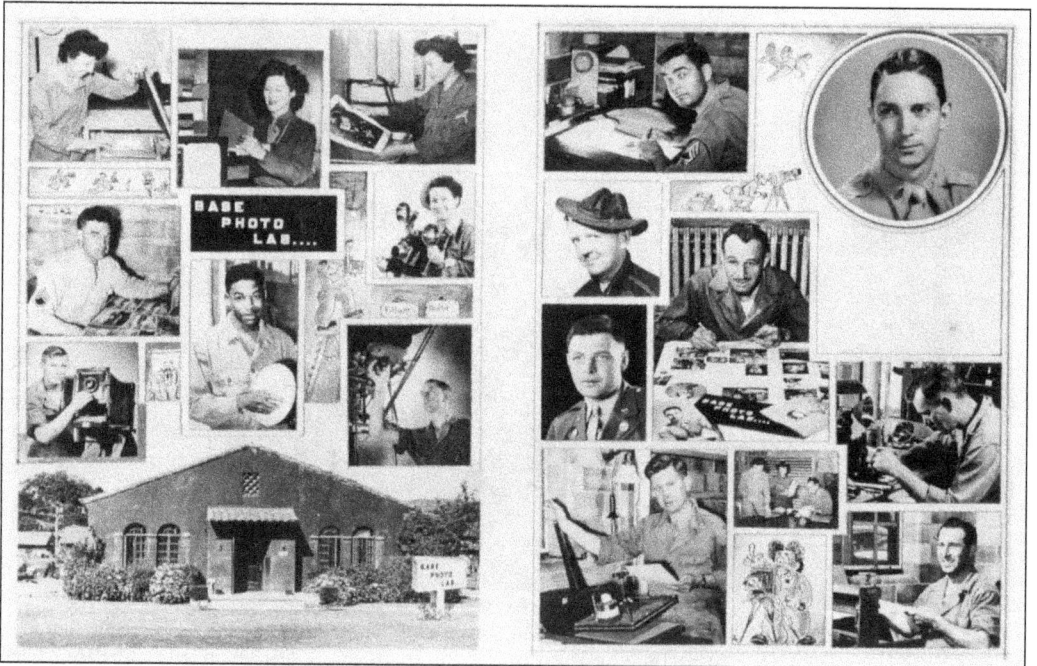

This yearbook page was printed and used as a brochure to illustrate personnel and work of the base photo lab in 1943–1944.

Sgt. Carl Cope, NCO, of the base photo lab, is shown checking negatives as they dried. Below, Jack Cannon and Carl Cope work on a layout project at the base photo lab in 1944.

Squadron W of the 460th AAF base unit of the Women's Army Auxiliary Corps (WAAC) poses for a group photograph in March 1944. Besides their regularly scheduled duties, the Women's Auxiliary Corps Squadron played a very important service by tending to the injured in the hospital—from writing letters for patients to helping maintain morale. Women also served as Women Airforce Service Pilots (WASP) at Hamilton and flew supplies and transports along the West Coast during wartime.

The post engineer department posed for a group photograph in April 1946. The department was composed of men and women, both civilian and military personnel. Included in the department was a versatile sheet-metal shop that manufactured everything from kitchen hoods to gutters on the edge of buildings. The Hamilton Field paper reported on March 3, 1945, that the metal workers were "asked to duplicate the former Air Force insignia for an unusual white and blue floral arrangement, and their media is galvanized iron, stainless steel, and copper."

A member of the chemical warfare service department demonstrates the use of a flame thrower, which, according to base chemical warfare officer Capt. Ernest Knoll in September 1944, would "eliminate pillboxes, burn out machine gun nests, set tanks on fire, and stop the enemy dead in his tracks."

All flight plans were processed through Hangar No. 7, base operations, and all flights in and out of Hamilton were controlled from the tower. Visiting aircraft was met—anytime of the day or night— and parked, then secured by the ground crew until departure. This photograph was taken on May 31, 1949, and shows that the hangars had yet to be repainted after years of camouflage.

B-36 bombers are shown in formation over Hamilton AAF during the 1948 Armed Forces Day. These bombers, too large to be based at Hamilton, made a special appearance for the event.

Even the officers' quarters did not escape the camouflage paintbrush. Captain Nurse's original plan called for homes for 62 married commissioned officers, and the houses were of many different types, ranging from one story, to one-and-a-half story, to two stories. There were two-story duplex quarters to accommodate 70 married noncommissioned officers of the first three grades, with their families.

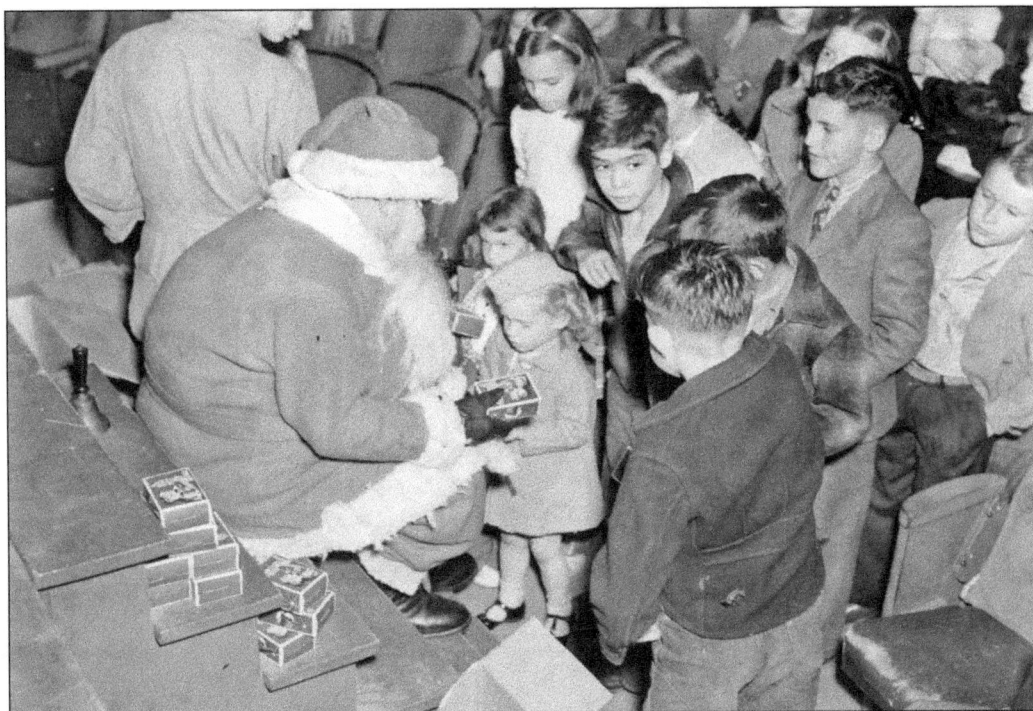

A group of Hamilton's children visit with Santa in December 1944. One of the many activities provided to the families stationed at Hamilton were holiday parties.

Families of the men and women stationed at Hamilton used the base's nondenominational chapel for worship services, which were held weekly for Protestant, Catholic, and Jewish congregations.

With the population of Hamilton growing through the 1940s, a temporary barracks building was turned into a second base movie theater.

The athletic fields are shown here, photographed in 1949. Special importance was placed on physical activity because the soldier had to be in excellent condition to perform well during any unexpected emergency. Team sports were often organized, with one platoon playing against another.

One of the many activities available to service men was bowling. An unidentified soldier was photographed at the bowling alley in 1947. The base gym had an attached bowling alley and was photographed on March 25, 1947.

The enlisted men's service club was a popular get-together place for informal games, dances, playing pool, and bingo, among other activities.

The hobby and art room of the service club became a popular place. Instruction in art was given each Tuesday and Friday for those who wished to participate.

Pfc. Frederick Falts, former commercial artist, added the finishing touches to a portrait in the hobby and art room of the service club, September 18, 1944.

This is the well-equipped library, photographed in October 1944, where troops could read for relaxation or do research work.

3636 401 BU 25 Mar 47 Food bar. NCO Club

Above, two enlisted men eat at the NCO club food bar, March 25, 1947. Below, men shoot pool at the NCO club, where the noncommissioned officers socialized outside of the mess hall.

3590 401 BU 25 Mar 47 NCO Club scene

This photograph shows the rear of the interdenominational chapel, the enlisted men's swimming pool and the tennis courts. Compare the photograph to the mural below.

This original mural of a day in the life of Hamilton Field was painted by Sgt. Paul Lantz in 1944. Sergeant Lantz enlisted in the U.S. Army in 1942 where he experienced action in the South Pacific. His duties included illustrator for the U.S. Army.

To keep morale high among the troops at Hamilton, the special services unit provided free shows in the outdoor amphitheater. USA Camp Shows, as well as local talent and professional entertainers from San Francisco, appeared regularly in the amphitheater. On September 30, 1944, screen actress Betty Hutton and her troop gave a surprise performance at the amphitheater before going overseas on a USO-sponsored tour of the Pacific theaters of war.

The USO Air Transport Command (ATC) band, along with an unidentified entertainer, performed at the Hamilton amphitheater in 1943.

Joe E. Brown, a popular movie comic, brought his troop to entertain at Hamilton on April 23, 1943.

Sgt. Joe Stabile, left, and his ATC band played an important part in keeping morale high at Hamilton Field. To the right at the piano is Lt. Don Mousted, who arranged the band music when not flying transports. The band played for dances in the evenings in addition to their regular duties. This meant that these men often worked six days a week from 8:00 a.m. to midnight.

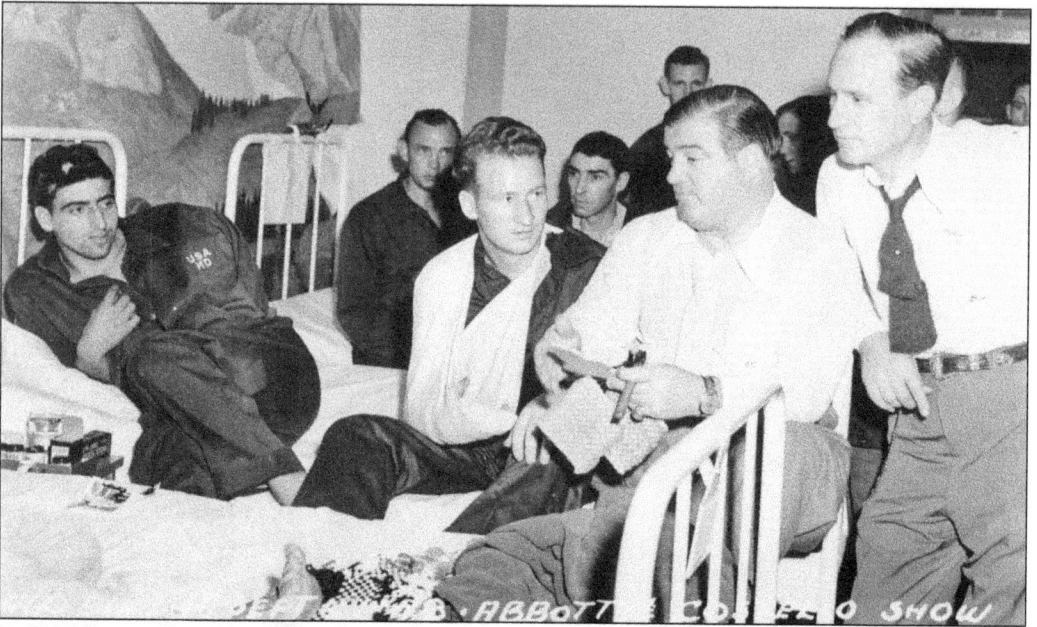

Bud Abbott and Lou Costello tour the evacuee wards of the debarkation hospital at Hamilton Field, September 14, 1944. With them in the picture are Pvt. Fran Donadio (left) and Pvt. Neil Roseboom (center). In August 1944, Hamilton's hospital was designated as an Army Airfield (AAF) regional and debarkation hospital. Here the wounded from the AAF, infantry, mechanized cavalry, antiaircraft squadrons, as well as a few from the U.S. Navy and U.S. Marines, were treated.

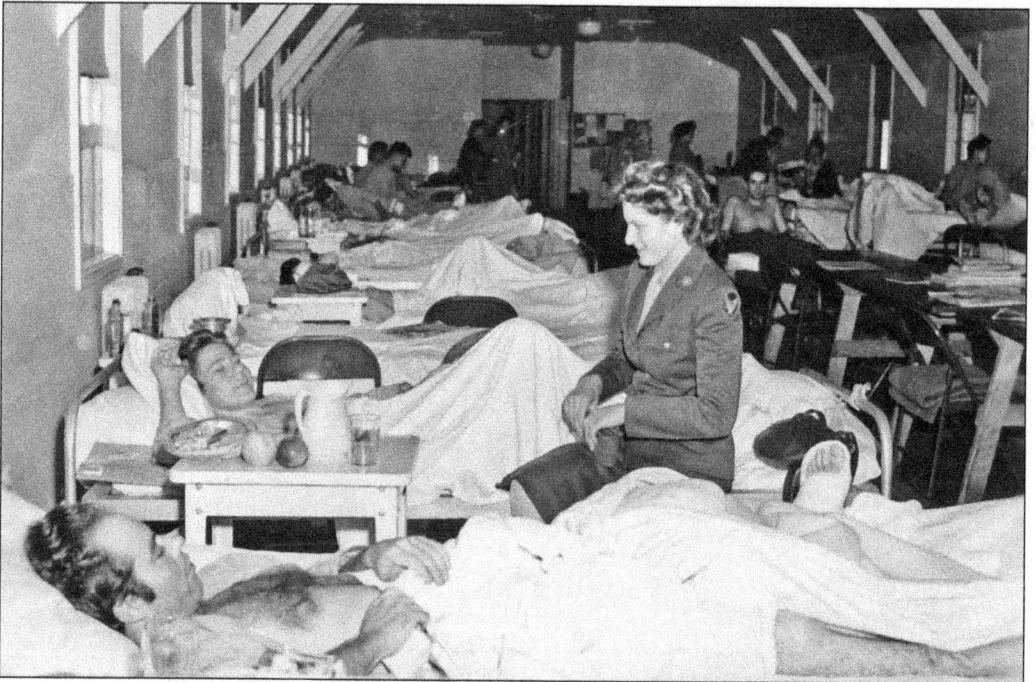

Pvt. Bryan McDaniel and Pvt. Lloyd Chustz are seen here with Pvt. Helen Becker at the debarkation hospital, August 13, 1944. Patients would remain at Hamilton for days or a few weeks before being sent to hospitals nearer their homes.

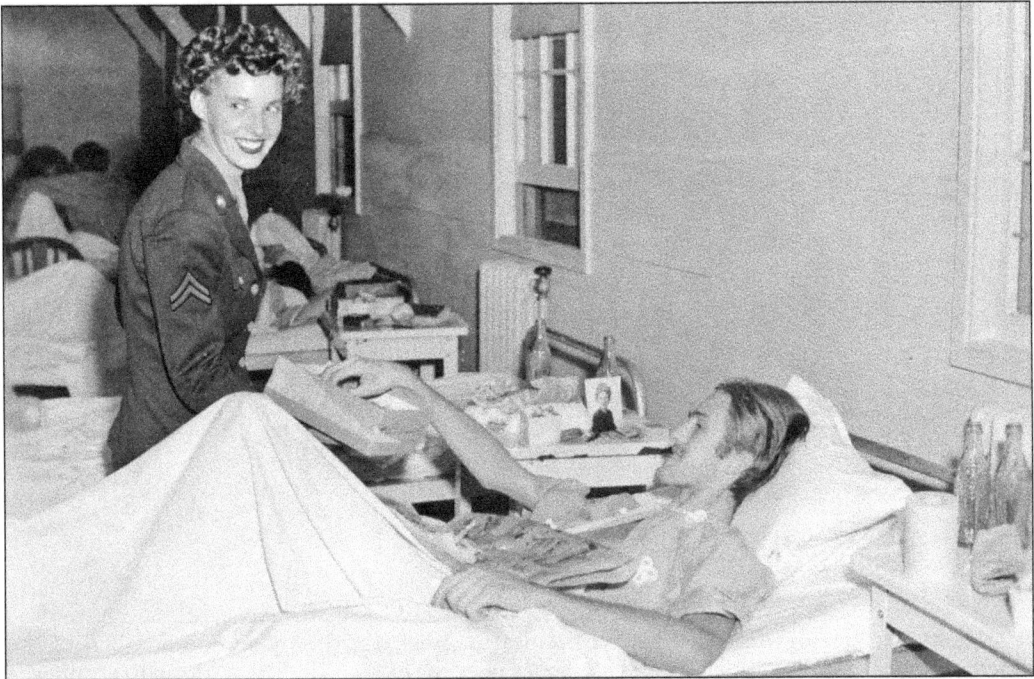

Cpl. Jackie Haldeman, WAC cook, distributes homemade cookies to Pvt. LaVerne Huick in the debarkation hospital on August 13, 1944. During that month, an influx of servicemen who had fought in Saipan were treated at Hamilton.

The San Rafael Elk's Club entertained 50 evacuees from Hamilton's debarkation hospital on September 19, 1944. Because of the large number of wounded and the length of their stay, a new hospital recreation building, with an arts and skills shop, was built on the hill above the wards overlooking the whole field. This new building was dubbed an air base-in-miniature, as it provided basic services for the patients who could not have access to the regular base.

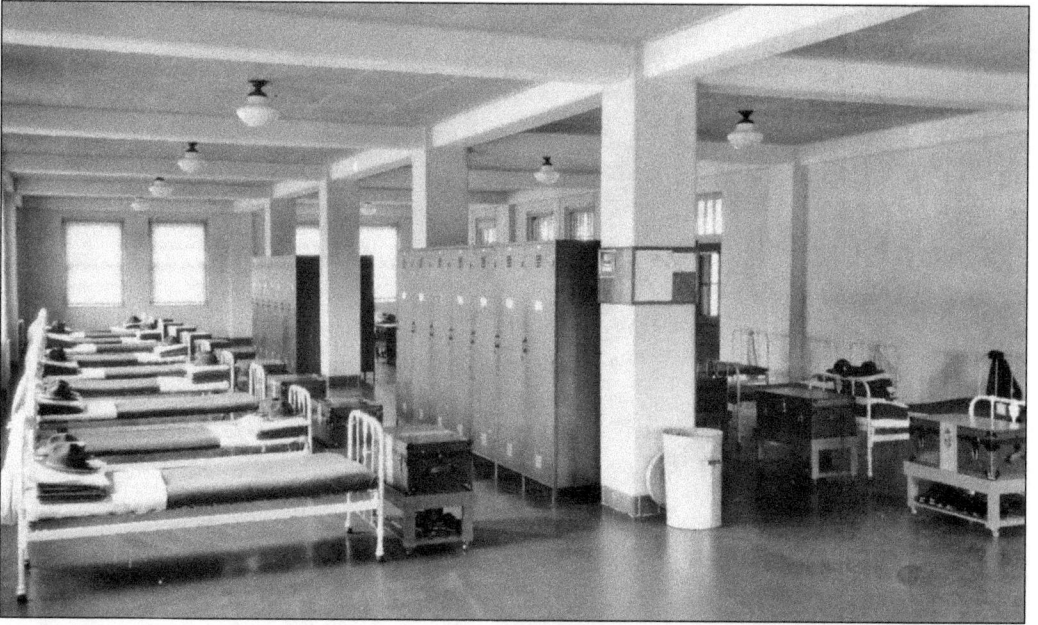

A challenge for Hamilton's debarkation hospital in 1944 was the increasing numbers of the evacuated battle injured, which caused an urgent need for more beds. The solution to ensure the safety and comfort of these men was to convert Barracks Nos. 422 and 424, two of the permanent barracks built in the 1930s, to house the wounded. This photograph shows the interior of the barracks as it would have been used when occupied by the regular squadrons.

Sergeant Chambers, Corporal Armstead, and Sergeant Harriman moved from their original barracks. Squadron A of the 460th Bombardment Unit moved from their barracks to temporary quarters.

Personnel from Barracks No. 422 loaded their personal equipment and the barracks furniture onto a truck to move to their temporary quarters. Below, they are shown arriving and unloading their equipment at their new quarters.

A hospital patient is carried on a litter to his new quarters in Barracks No. 422.

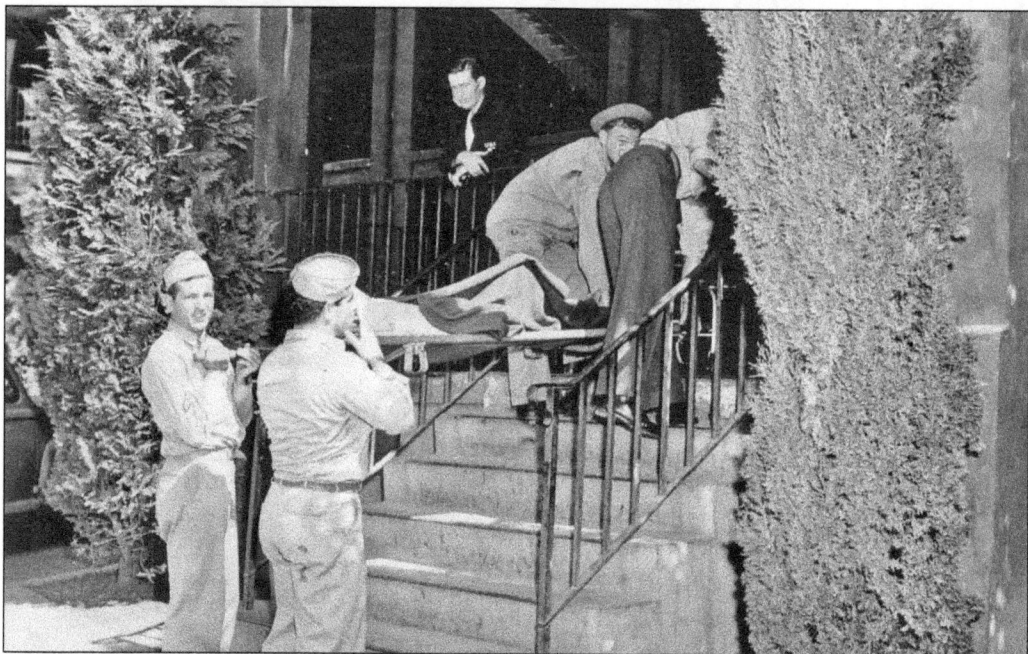

Pvt. John McCrery is carried into his new quarters in Barracks No. 422. According to the plan for occupying the barracks, litter patients occupied the first floor, ambulatory were on the other two, and the basement was used for supplies. The move was documented photographically on August 25, 1944.

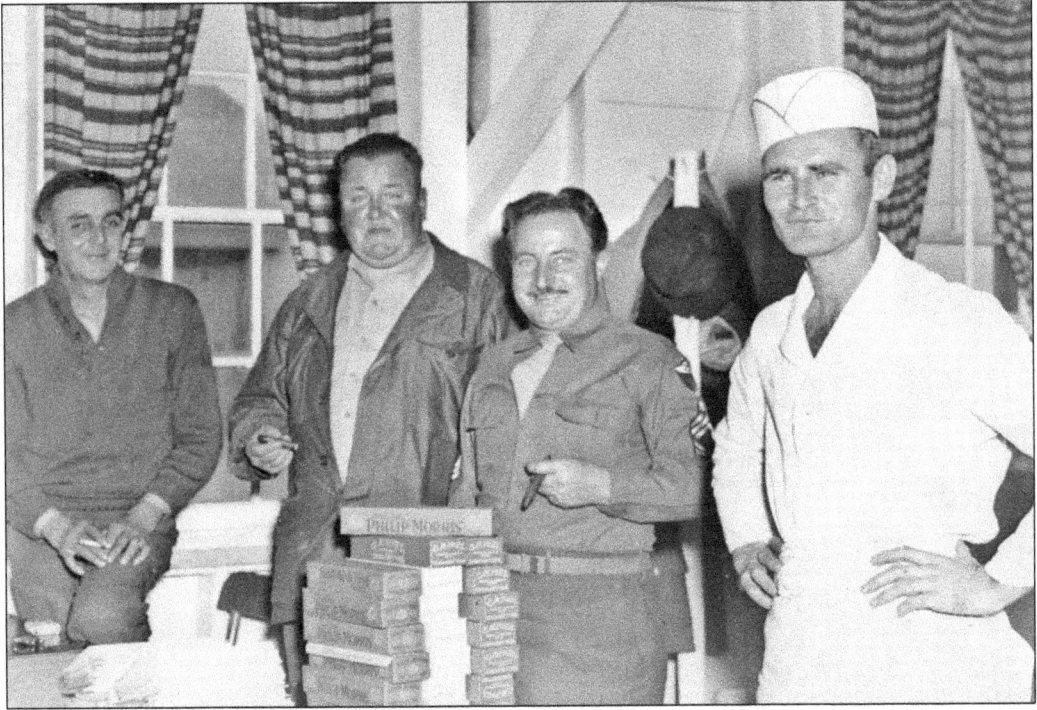

For Christmas 1944, cigarettes were passed out to all of the patients of the debarkation hospital as a special holiday treat.

Barracks No. 424 is in camouflage and decorated for Christmas, most likely photographed in the late 1940s. At that time, the barracks was home to the 78th Fighter Group's maintenance supply group, for which the insignia can be seen over the doorway.

In March 1945, nurses who had been prisoners of war landed at Hamilton Field and were greeted with a heroes' welcome. The *Novato Advance* reported that "Hamilton Field, which has become used to seeing heroes return home, wore its heart on its sleeve for a brief half hour and went completely wild over the sixty-eight 'Angels of Bataan,' Army nurses liberated from Japanese prisoner of war camps a month ago. Nothing was too good for the nurses. Already the former second lieutenants were wearing silver bars, the first lieutenants their captain's insignia. They'd been promoted in Honolulu and been awarded the Bronze Star. Top ranking flight nurses flew with them in the new luxury C-54 and they rode into San Francisco only three to a staff car, in complete comfort."

This parade was for Capt. Samuel Grashio, who returned to the United States on February 4, 1944, after escaping from the Japanese. Many war heroes from the Pacific theater arrived at Hamilton AAF as their first stop on their way home and were given enthusiastic and grateful welcomes.

In April 1945, Pres. Harry S. Truman arrives at Hamilton to attend the United Nations Conference for International Organization in San Francisco.

President Truman is greeted on the Hamilton tarmac. Representatives from many nations to the United Nations conference in San Francisco landed and departed from Hamilton AAF between April 15–25, 1945.

One of the first acts performed by President Truman upon arrival at Hamilton was to visit the evacuation hospital.

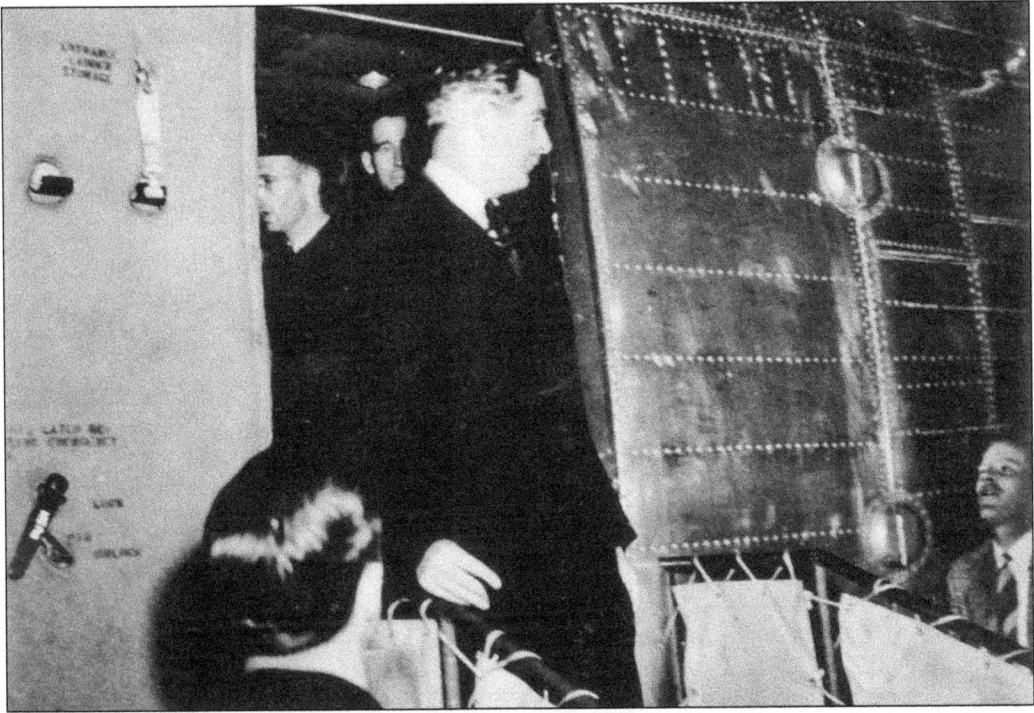

Sir Anthony Eden, one of Great Britain's delegates to the United Nations charter meetings in San Francisco, arrives at Hamilton in April 1945.

Gen. Omar Bradley was greeted at Hamilton AAF on October 2, 1946. General Bradley was one of the most famous U.S. generals during World War II. After the war, he headed the Veterans Administration for two years. He is credited with doing much to improve its health-care system and with helping veterans receive their educational benefits under the GI Bill of Rights.

The U.S. Secretary of War, Robert P. Patterson (right), was greeted at Hamilton on October 2, 1946. He posed with two injured airmen and famed fighter pilot Capt. Eddie Rickenbacker (second from right).

Capt. Eddie Rickenbacker (center), World War I ace fighter pilot and Medal of Honor recipient, arrives at Hamilton Field to talk with pilots in 1946. Rickenbacker was also a famed race car driver and automotive designer, as well as a government consultant in military matters and a pioneer in air transportation.

Four

FROM GROWTH TO DECOMMISSIONING

The Color Guard stands at attention in front of the last Hamilton main gate in the early 1950s (there were three main gates constructed over the years of base activity). Renamed Hamilton Air Force Base with the creation of the U.S. Air Force (USAF) in 1947, the base served as an important part in the protection of San Francisco and the entire West Coast against invasion.

Gen. Hap Arnold, who had retired to Sonoma, California, passed away on January 15, 1950, from a cardiac condition. A ceremony took place at Hamilton AFB in his honor as his casket was transported for burial. Arnold Drive in Sonoma is named in his honor.

General Arnold's casket was loaded onto a C-54 military transport plane at Hamilton AFB for transport to Washington, D.C., for burial at Arlington National Cemetery in January 1950. General Arnold became chief of staff for the U.S. Air Force in 1941 but maintained quarters at Hamilton for the duration of his life.

A T-33A Shooting Star jet trainer aircraft is attached to a suppressor on the tarmac at Hamilton AFB in the early 1950s. The T-33A two-seat jet was designed for training pilots who were qualified to fly propeller-driven aircraft. It was used from its inception in the late 1940s onward by the U.S. Air Force. These aircraft, via other modifications and additions, remain in service worldwide today, despite their vintage.

Flight mechanics and staff team gather in front of fighter plane engines, photographed at Hamilton AFB in 1951.

A Hamilton-based formation of F-86D Sabre aircraft was photographed over northern California in the mid-1950s. The F-86D was flown by the 496th Fighter-Interceptor Squadron in 1953–1954, and by the 325th Fighter-Interceptor Squadron in 1954–1955. The 325th squadron sponsored the Sabre Knights aerial demonstration team while at Hamilton AFB.

The F-89 Scorpion was flown by the 84th Fighter Interceptor Squadron at Hamilton AFB during 1951–1952. Equipped with J35 turbojets, the F-89 was designed with an impressive (at that time) 1,300-mile range to intercept incoming enemy bombers.

A development from the two-seater T-33 Shooting Star trainer aircraft, the Lockheed F-94 was the U.S. Air Force's first operational jet-powered, all-weather interceptor aircraft.

An F-104 aircraft is prepared at Hamilton AFB for shipment to Taiwan in 1958. The Lockheed F-104 Starfighter was an American single-engine, high-performance, supersonic interceptor aircraft that served with the USAF from 1958 until 1967. The first unit of F-104A's to become operational in the United States was the 83rd Fighter Interceptor Squadron at Hamilton AFB in February 1958.

In October 1958, twelve F-104 aircraft from the 83rd Fighter Interceptor Squadron were loaded onto a C-124 carrier aircraft in preparation to be in service at Taeyan Air Base, Taiwan, where they supported the Quemoy Crisis. The F-104A initially served briefly with the USAF Air Defense Command as an interceptor, although neither its range nor armament was well suited for that role, and it had no all-weather capability.

An official Hamilton AFB press release accompanied this 1960 photograph. It read: "GUARDIANS OF FREEDOM . . . Flights of Mach-busting F-104 Starfighters from Hamilton Air Force Base will be in the air continuously on Armed Forces Day, Saturday, May 21. The Starfighters will be used to repel mock attacks on the cities of San Francisco and Oakland."

The McDonnell F-101B was flown by the 84th Fighter Interceptor Squadron at Hamilton AFB from 1955 to 1968. This plane, once some of its fire control systems were modified, proved to be an excellent interceptor aircraft. The dual-seat F-101F trainer was also flown at Hamilton AFB. The F-101B was used by the U.S. Air Force until the Convair F-106A Delta Dart replaced it in service in 1968.

An F-106A, flown by the 84th Fighter Interceptor Squadron, prepares for flight on the Hamilton AFB tarmac. After replacing the F-101B in service, the F-106A was considered one of the best all-weather interceptor aircraft ever engineered. It served from the 1960s until 1987.

The U.S. Military selected many modified Convair-Liner airplanes for a variety of tasks. The Convair T-29 began service as the primary Air Force training aircraft in the early 1950s. This aircraft could accommodate a crew of four (pilot, co-pilot, and two instructors) and 16 students.

The Douglas C-47 Skytrain, photographed here in August 1947, is a transport aircraft that was developed from the Douglas DC-3 airliner. It was used extensively by the Allies during World War II as a troop and cargo carrier, and remained in frontline operations through the 1950s. It was also part of the 349th Troop Carrier Reserve Wing.

The 349th Troop Carrier Wing, Medium, was re-designated by the U.S. Air Force reserve unit at Hamilton AFB in 1957, and flew the Fairchild C-119 Flying Boxcar. The wing was ordered to active duty in October 1962 during the Cuban Missile Crisis; it remained active until the cessation of the crisis on November 28, 1962.

The 349th Troop Carrier Wing, Medium, was again re-designated the 349th Military Airlift Wing in June 1966, when the unit was moved to military airlift command. They flew the Douglas C-124 Globemaster II, photographed at Hamilton AFB in the late 1950s. During the Vietnam War, this unit ferried tons of cargo to the U.S. forces throughout Southeast Asia, the Pacific, and even to Europe and the Middle East.

The 78th Fighter Wing
commanders and staff gather
for a group photograph
in 1960. The wing was
activated at Hamilton
AFB in 1948 and was
active at the base, with
the exception of the years
1952–1956, until 1969.

The *Novato Advance* photographed personnel at Hamilton AFB in the late 1950s. These Pararescuemen are U.S. Air Force Special Operations Command and Air Combat Command operatives who are trained in the rescue and treatment of personnel in humanitarian and combat environments. They are among only a few units in the U.S. Air Force to wear a beret, which is a symbol of their elite status. Below, a fighter pilot prepares for a training flight.

A photographer from the *Novato Advance* photographed a parachute jump during a training exercise over Hamilton AFB in the late 1950s.

An official Hamilton AFB press release accompanied this April 1960 photograph. It reads, "SUPERHUMAN SECURITY IN THE SUPERSONIC AGE . . . The Air Force is insuring its modern weapons of defense with one of the oldest safeguards known to man—THE SENTRY DOG. Patrolling security areas, teams of their dogs and their handlers, such as Kim and A/1C David R. Turcotte, act as a bulwark against any would-be intruder."

An official Hamilton AFB press release accompanied this June 1959 photograph. It reads, "THREAT TO INTRUDER—OR PHOTOGRAPHER! Lancer, Air Force canine guard, and A/2C Larry T. Flom guard their post at Hamilton AFB, Calif. The photographer, A/3C John E. Brunner, was knocked down, but uninjured, as Airman Flom pulled up sharply on Lancer's leash."

The setting sun is a backdrop to the canine guard and his handler, photographed in 1960 at Hamilton AFB.

A Hamilton-based F-86D Sabre of the 78th Fighter Group was named the "City of Novato" in 1960.

Hamilton's main gate, shown here in the late 1950s, was decorated and festively lit up for the holiday season.

This aerial photograph, taken on January 7, 1949, shows the administration building painted white, while the remaining buildings on base were still in camouflage. Through World War II, activity at Hamilton Field had continued at the same feverish pace that had begun with Pearl Harbor. The wounded poured in from overseas, men and material were rushed to combat zones, and everyone was geared to a wartime effort. When the war ended in 1945, the immediate result was confusion. Combat crews on their way overseas were returned to the mainland with no prior notice to the base. Administrative and personnel function were also thrown into general confusion. Morale also suffered when families arriving in the area to be with the men returning from overseas could find no suitable housing. The base and the local community did their best, but they could not meet this need. Many complaints resulted because of the substandard housing on the base and in surrounding communities.

In this photograph of the base hospital, taken in the 1950s, it is evident how much building occurred in the years from its construction (compared to the photograph on page 38). Many additional structures were built to accommodate the thousands of patients who were treated during World War II, as well as additional barracks to house the growing population of Hamilton AFB during the 1940s and 1950s.

The 200 Area (an address designation on base) was where officers' housing was situated, and contained three- and four-bedroom houses that were built in the 1930s as part of the original vision for Hamilton Field.

This three-bedroom home was also in the 200 Area of Hamilton Field and was among the original housing there.

This building in the 500 Area of Hamilton Field was composed of three-bedroom townhouses for senior noncommissioned officers and was part of the original 1930s architecture.

100

These apartments, in the Capehart Housing area on base, were constructed in the 1950s and consisted of three-bedrooms units for enlisted personnel. Pictured below, the one-level duplexes, also in the Capehart Housing area on base, had three to four bedrooms.

Rafael Village was a housing area constructed just east of Hamilton Field. The development was intended as family housing. Both of these photographs are of the Wherry model, which was a two-bedroom duplex intended for enlisted personnel.

In May 1965, Hamilton Air Force Base was rededicated on its 30th anniversary. A luncheon was held at the Hamilton NCO club, and the guest of honor was Eleanor Arnold (at the center of the main table on the left), widow of the first and only general of the U.S. Air Force. General Arnold had made the first dedication speech for the installation in 1935.

Eleanor Arnold cuts the cake to celebrate the 30-year rededication ceremony for Hamilton. To the left is Maj. Gen. Carroll W. McColpin, commander of the 28th Air Division, and to the right is Col. Ralph M. Wanderer Jr., commander of Hamilton AFB, as well as Richard Nave, president of the Novato Chamber of Commerce.

Highlights of the all-day 30-year rededication ceremonies and festivities at Hamilton included the presentation of a permanent plaque by Marin County Board of Supervisor's chairman, Peter H. Behr (left), to Col. Ralph M. Wanderer Jr., commander of Hamilton AFB, as well as a flyover by Hamilton-based F-104 fighter planes.

A large crowd waits in anticipation for Pres. Richard Nixon's arrival at Hamilton AFB in 1970. Below, President Nixon and First Lady Pat Nixon arrive at Hamilton AFB and wave to the crowds.

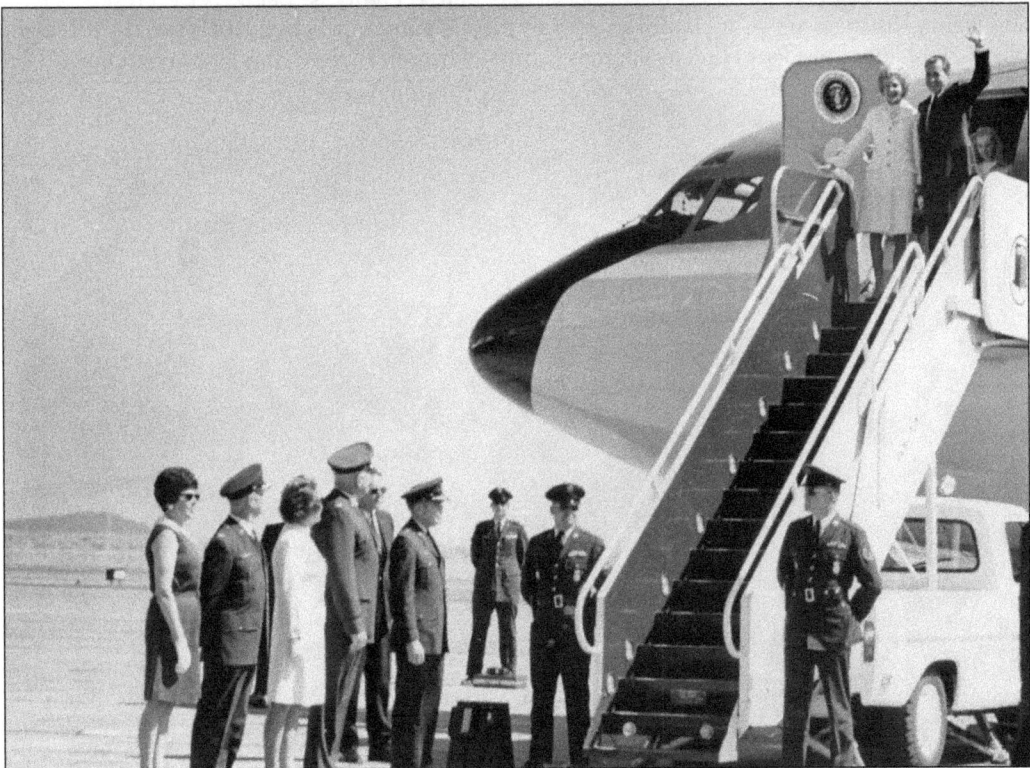

President Nixon greets members of the service as well as civilians. Below, Vice President Ford and Henry Kissinger arrive at Hamilton AFB in 1970. Hamilton was frequently used by President Nixon, and later President Ford, as an arrival point when en route to Bay Area engagements.

COMMANDERS OF HAMLITON

HOWARD B. NURSE, Capt. Q.M.C.
CONSTRUCTING QUARTERMASTER
APRIL 1931-JUNE 1935

DON L. HUTCHINS, Capt. A.C.
27 JUN- 33-4 DEC 34

CLARENCE L. TINKER, Maj. A.C.
5 DEC 34-8 DEC 36

DAVENPORT JOHNSON, Col. A.C.
16 DEC 36-25 FEB 38

JOHN F. CURRY, Col. A.C.
12 APR 38-27 OCT 40

MILLARD F. HARMON, Brig. Gen. A.C.
22 NOV 40-16 JAN 41

MICHAEL F. DAVIS, Col. A.C.
17 JAN 41-16 JUN 41 & 25 JUL 41-30 NOV 41

WILLIAM O. RYAN, Brig. Gen. A.C.
17 JUN 41-24 JUL 41

LOTHA A. SMITH, Col. A.C.
4 DEC 41-31 MAR 43

GEORGE F. KINZIE, Col. A.C.
1 APR 43-30 APR 44

CHARLES R. MELIN, Col. A.C.
1 MAY 44-1 OCT 45

HOWARD E. ENGLER, Col. A.C.
2 NOV 45-12 AUG 46

WENTWORTH GOSS, Col. A.C.
12 AUG 46-10 OCT 47

Although Hamilton is misspelled in this review of the Commanders of Hamilton that was produced in 1973, this Hamilton yearbook page remains an enduring tribute to the commanders who served through nearly five decades of war and peace.

107

GEORGE L. USHER, Brig. Gen. USAF
11 OCT 47-31 MAR 50

GEORGE H. STEEL, Col. USAF
1 APR 50-11 MAR 51

BRIAN O'NEILL, Col. USAF
13 MAR 51-30 JUN 51

JAMES W. ANDREW, Col. USAF
1 JUL 51-3 FEB 52

FRED D. STEVERS, Col. USAF
4 FEB 52-10 JUL 52

GEORGE F. ANDERSON, Col. USAF
10 JUL 52-9 JUL 55

WILTON H. EARLE, Col. USAF
9 JUL 55-26 JUL 57

GEORGE F. CEULEERS, Col. USAF
27 JUL 57-16 JUL 60

HARVEY E. HENDERSON, Col. USAF
17 JUL 60-12 MAY 62

WILLIAM F. BARNS, Col. USAF
12 MAY 62-1 JUL 62

WILLIAM S. HARRELL, Col. USAF
1 JUL 62-1 APR 63

BRYANT Y. ANDERSON, Col. USAF
1 APR 63-25 JUN 64

Shown here are Commanders of Hamilton, continued, from 1947 to 1964.

RALPH M. WANDERER, JR., Col. USAF
1 JUL 64-1 APR 66

CHARLES L. PRAUL, Col. USAF
1 APR 66-9 SEP 68

MICHAEL J. STUBLAREC, Col. USAF
9 SEP 68-28 AUG 69

MERVYN M. TAYLOR, Col USAF
28 AUG 69-8 OCT 69

LEE A. SARTER, JR., Col USAF
8 OCT 69-1 AUG 71

VERMONT GARRISON, Col. USAF
1 AUG 71-28 FEB 73

R. R. MELTON, Col. USAF
28 FEB 73-1 OCT 73

Only one more commander, Brig. Gen. William G. Hathaway, served at Hamilton following this publication. General Hathaway served from October 1, 1973, until the base decommissioning in 1974.

A retreat ceremony for an unspecified event is held at the flagpole in front of Building 500. In 1974, the airfield was transferred to the U.S. Army as Hamilton Army Airfield, the housing was transferred to the U.S. Navy, and a 411-acre parcel of the base was transferred to the General Services Administration for public sale.

Five

OPEN HOUSES
AND AIR SHOWS

The general public and families of those stationed at Hamilton visit the base for Armed Forces Day in 1948. Planes not usually seen at Hamilton were showcased, along with the regular squadrons. For this day in 1948, visitors watch a B-36 flyby with a B-29 Superfortress on the tarmac; both planes were too large to regularly be housed at Hamilton AFB. Early open houses included demonstrations of cargo drops by C-47s, and many of the bomber and early jet fighter planes flew in formation, or flew over the amazed crowds with open bomb bays. Open houses and air shows continued through the 1970s, when the base was decommissioned. From 1987 to 1990, the Wings of Victory air show continued that tradition and proved to be an exceptional event, thanks to the help of countless volunteers, civilians, and retired service personnel from Novato and Hamilton communities.

Members of the public visit a Northrop P-61 Black Widow, its engine removed for maintenance, during the 1948 Armed Forces Day open house.

Visitors peruse jets and missiles during the 1948 Armed Forces Day open house. This photograph was taken at Hangar No. 7; the building was still painted in camouflage from World War II years.

Open houses at Hamilton AFB came about because the postwar housing boom in the 1950s was bringing local residents closer to the airfield. After World War II, Hamilton continued to be a major base and training facility. New jet planes were stationed at the base, and nearby residents began to complain about jets screaming through the air. The U.S. Air Force invited residents to an open house to improve public relations. People could see up close the innovative designs that followed World War II into the arms race. Besides generating goodwill, the open houses offered opportunities for participation with local businesses and served as an enticement for new recruits to join the U.S. Air Force. A 1958 open house and air show attracted 25,000 visitors.

Hamilton AFB open houses in the 1950s introduced the public to new developments in airplane design, such as faster-than-sound flying that produced sonic booms. An article in the May 13, 1957, edition of the *Novato Advance* reassured readers and residents that the boom "will not be dangerous for spectators, nor will it create property damage." These photographs of open houses from the 1960s and 1970s show a variety of airplanes parked on the tarmac, from propeller-driven planes to the most advanced fighter and interceptor jets of the day.

By the 1970s, Hamilton AFB open houses were grand affairs, usually coinciding with Armed Forces Day. Visitors could see displays by all of the branches of service, watch dazzling performances by the Air Force Thunderbirds and the Golden Knights Parachute Team, see firefighting demonstrations, and give close-up inspections of military and vintage airplanes.

All ages of visitors were enthralled by the opportunity at open houses to get up close to, and even climb into, fighter jet planes. Also on display during the open houses were missiles and weaponry. The photograph below from the 1950s shows a missile with signage underscoring the fact that it is an inert atomic model.

The local community participated at the Hamilton AFB open houses as well. School color guards and drill teams prepared programs, and exhibits by the Red Cross, California Highway Patrol, veterans, aircraft modelers, and racers provided plenty of opportunities to learn about the military and civilian contributions to aviation history.

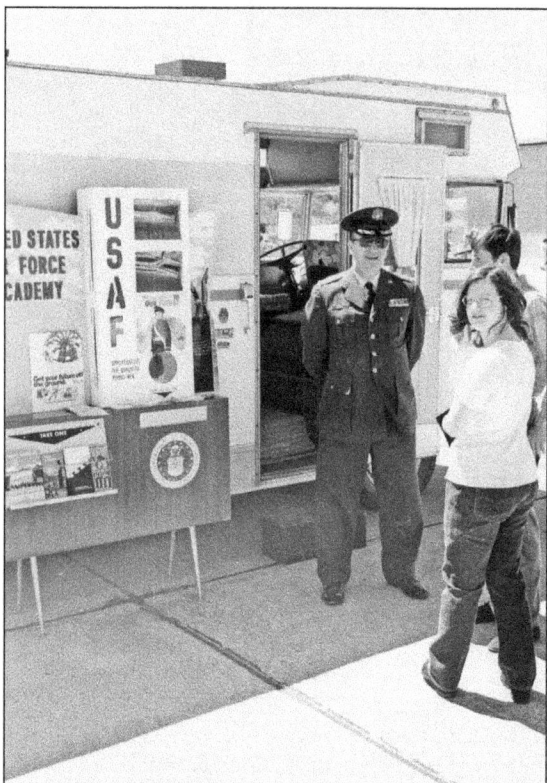

All of the armed forces recruited at Hamilton open houses and air shows. Here a U.S. Air Force recruiter talks to visitors during the 1973 open house.

This booth at the Hamilton open house in 1973 helped keep alive the issue of those service people who were Missing in Action (MIA) and raise awareness.

In 1980–1981, another kind of open house was instituted at Hamilton. Refugees from Vietnam were processed at the transit center run by the Switzerland-based Intergovernmental Committee for Migration (ICOM) at Hamilton AFB. Even though the base had been decommissioned in 1975, the facilities were used for this event as thousands of refugees immigrated to the United States. (Courtesy of Lisa Hoytt.)

Vietnamese refugees were airlifted to Oakland International Airport and San Francisco International Airport, and then were bused to Hamilton AFB to be processed before being sent to their new homes throughout the United States. Buses arrived at Hamilton and members of ICOM greeted people as they disembarked and entered the barracks. (Courtesy of Lisa Hoytt.)

ICOM representatives welcomed refugees and briefly oriented them to the process of their brief stay of a few days at Hamilton AFB. Supplies, such as bedding and toiletries, were distributed to families. (Courtesy of Lisa Hoytt.)

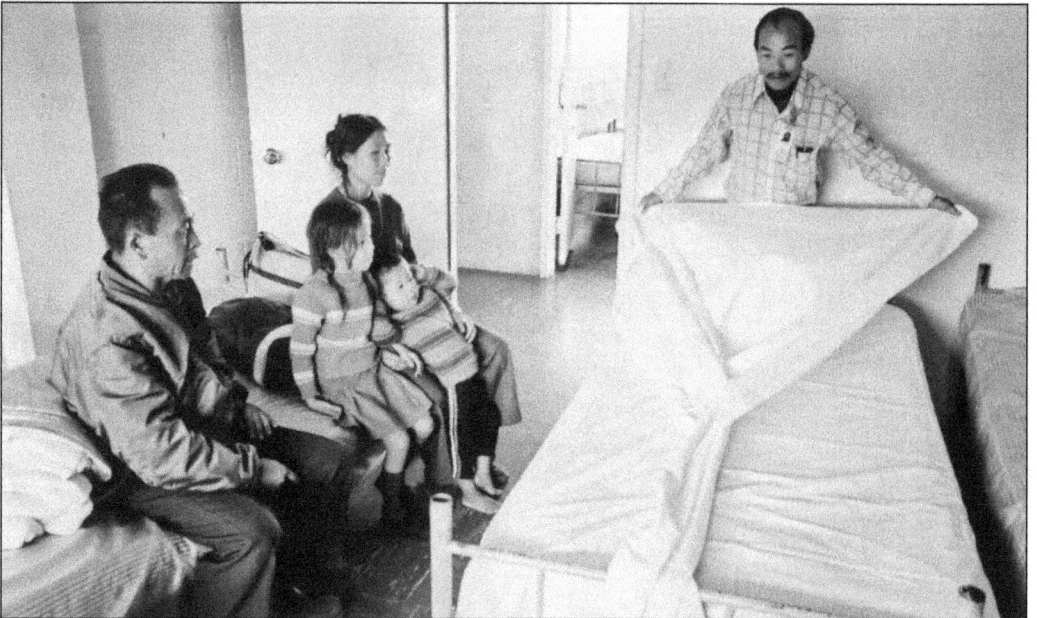

A family is shown their temporary quarters in a former barracks at Hamilton AFB. This ICOM representative helped orient families and helped them settle in for their brief stay. As of November 4, 1982, about 34,500 refugees had been processed at Hamilton before going to their new residences all across the United States, from Oregon to Minnesota to Pennsylvania. (Courtesy of Lisa Hoytt.)

Six

HAMILTON TODAY

Developers of Hamilton Field reconstructed the main gate in the Spanish Eclectic style to blend with the historic architecture. Upon entering Hamilton today, the visitor will notice beautiful landscaping, neighborhood open spaces, parks, and new residential and commercial developments. In 1998, certain buildings on the former base were designated the Hamilton Army Airfield Discontiguous Historic District by the National Park Service's National Trust for Historic Preservation. Some of those buildings, including the administration building, known as Building 500, and the original firehouse have been preserved and restored. Others sit empty and are in need of restoration, and still others have been integrated into the active and successful housing and business park development that illustrate a successful base reuse plan. The officers' swimming pool and some other buildings on the base are owned by the City of Novato and are utilized for assorted recreation and community services for the benefit of the Hamilton and greater Novato communities. All photographs in this chapter were taken by Novato Historical Guild member Ron Vela in February 2008.

Building 500 was the original headquarters building of the base and was where the war room was located. The war room was located on the second floor; its intricately detailed window can be seen above the entrance door. Today the building has been refurbished to its original glory, but instead of housing plans of war, it serves as the Novato Art Center.

The restored lobby of Building 500 has ceiling beams that look like hand-carved and painted beams but are actually cast concrete. The building is now home to the City of Novato's Art Center, the Art League of Northern California, and the Marin Museum of Contemporary Art (MOCA) gallery. The building houses numerous artist studios, as do the cluster of small buildings surrounding it.

Hangar No. 6 now houses the South Novato Library and other businesses. The commercial development of most of the hangars, called Hamilton Landing, encompasses 800,000 square feet of leasing space. The business park includes a campus-type atmosphere with connecting walkways, palm trees, and outside seating. Some of the businesses that are housed in the hangars include Oracle, Birkenstock USA, Sony Pictures Image Works, the YMCA, Marin Community Foundation, the South Novato Library, U.S. Army Corps of Engineers, and Visual Concepts Entertainment, to name a few. There are more than 40 businesses now operating in the hangars that have been completed. The Coast Guard still maintains a presence on part of the base, including Hangars Nos. 1 and 2.

The control tower attached to Hangar No. 7 had deteriorated in the past few decades. It is currently being renovated and will be the centerpiece of the most current development project, to be completed by 2009. Recently ImageMovers Digital Studio, a subsidiary of Disney, announced plans to occupy the 90,000 square feet of Hangars Nos. 7 and 9.

The Novato Historical Guild, in partnership with the City of Novato, has been planning to open the Hamilton Field History Museum in the 1934 firehouse since the late 1990s. With the goal to open in 2009, the guild envisions a museum that would exhibit and collect Hamilton's artifacts, as well as serve as a community hub, where stories of the men and women who served, worked, and lived at Hamilton could be preserved.

The Bachelors Officers Quarters (BOQ) is, to this day, a grand structure with beautiful archways and intricate Spanish architecture. It also has a hilltop location with sweeping views of Hamilton and San Pablo Bay. Since the base was closed, ideas for its reuse have been proposed, including plans to renovate it as a hotel. Those plans never materialized, and now the building stands boarded and vacant.

The stately Hamilton hospital, in which so many servicemen, women, and their families were cared for, now sits abandoned and forgotten. Vandals have broken the glass throughout the building. Like the BOQ and the original theater, proposals for the reuse of the structures have been submitted, but as of the writing of this book, they are all among the buildings with uncertain futures, waiting to be rescued.

The *Novato Advance* reported in 1998, "A town grows at Hamilton." This panoramic photograph, taken 10 years later, shows that the residences and parks are complete. The three original barracks

After the redevelopment of Hamilton commenced, the result of the ambitious decision to return much of the property adjacent to San Pablo Bay to its original marshland state is now in process.

buildings can be seen among the housing developments at the right of the photograph, with the former hangars at the center.

In the largest West Coast restoration project ever attempted, levees have been built just east of the hangars, and the runways are now underwater.

Visit us at
arcadiapublishing.com